MW00713688

Penetration

Testing

The Ultimate 2021 Guide about Hacking Process & Kali Linux Installation. Defend Yourself from Wireless Hacking.

© Copyright 2021 - All rights reserved.

The content contained within this book may not be reproduced, duplicated or transmitted without direct written permission from the author or the publisher.

Under no circumstances will any blame or legal responsibility be held against the publisher, or author, for any damages, reparation, or monetary loss due to the information contained within this book. Either directly or indirectly.

Legal Notice:

This book is copyright protected. This book is only for personal use. You cannot amend, distribute, sell, use, quote or paraphrase any part, or the content within this book, without the consent of the author or publisher.

Disclaimer Notice:

Please note the information contained within this document is for educational and entertainment purposes only. All effort has been executed to present accurate, up to date, and reliable, complete information. No warranties of any kind are declared or implied. Readers acknowledge that the author is not engaging in the rendering of legal, financial, medical or professional advice. The content within this book has been derived from various sources. Please consult a licensed professional before attempting any techniques outlined in this book.

By reading this document, the reader agrees that under no circumstances is the author responsible for any losses, direct or indirect, which are incurred as a result of the use of information contained within this document, including, but not limited to, — errors, omissions, or inaccuracies.

Table of Contents

Introduction

The following chapters will discuss hacking in detail for beginners. We will introduce Linux along with commands that will help us understand better about bash language. We will then discuss about various tools in detail that belongs to kali Linux. We will now just give a rough introduction to hacking process so that you can have a comfortable mindset while reading this book.

Types of hackers:

In my understanding, hackers should be divided into two categories that is positive and evil. Decent hackers rely on their own knowledge to help system administrators identify vulnerabilities in the system and make the systems Perfect whereas evil hackers attack, invade, or do other things that are harmful to the network through various hacking skills. As they do things in an unethical way these people are called as Crackers instead of hackers.

Regardless of the type of hacker, their initial learning content will be the same as we discuss in this book and the basic skills are the same. Many people ask: "What do hackers do in peacetime?" Some people understand hackers as boring and repeating humans that do the same work every day. But that is just a misunderstanding. Hackers usually need a lot of time to learn.

In addition to learning, hackers should apply their knowledge to the real world. No matter what kind of work a hacker does, the fundamental purpose is nothing more than grasping what they have learned in practice

The hacker's behavior mainly includes the following:

First, learning technology:

Once new technologies on the Internet appear, hackers must learn immediately and master the technology in the shortest time. The mastery here is not a general understanding, but reading about the protocol like rfc and gain an in-depth understanding of the mechanics of this technology. Once a hacker stops learning, he can no more be a hacker.

The knowledge that primary hackers want to learn is more difficult because they have no foundation or any guidance so they have to learn a lot of basic content. However, today's Internet brings a lot of information to readers and can make beginners overwhelming. Therefore, beginners can't be greedy. They should try to find a book and their own complete textbooks, and learn step by step. Glad you find your book and are going to dive into it in few pages.

Second, disguise yourself:

Every move of the hacker will be recorded by the server, so the hacker must disguise himself so that the other party can't distinguish his true identity. This requires skilled skills to disguise his IP address, use the springboard to avoid tracking, and clean up the record. It also includes disturbing the other party's clues and cleverly avoiding the firewall.

Camouflage is a very basic skill that hackers need to be achieve. This is a big world for beginners, which means that beginners can't learn to pretend in a short time. So, I don't encourage beginners to use their own learning. Without Knowledge don't attack the network because once your own behavior is revealed, the ultimate harm is on yourself.

Third, the discovery of vulnerabilities:

Vulnerabilities are the most important information for hackers. Hackers should often learn the vulnerabilities discovered by others, and try to find unknown vulnerabilities themselves, and find valuable and exploitable vulnerabilities from a large number of vulnerabilities. Of course, their ultimate goal is to destroy or fix this vulnerability through vulnerabilities.

The hacker's obsession with finding loopholes is unimaginable. Their slogan says "breaking authority". A program with a vulnerability is like a festival for hackers and they would love to mess it up to create more backdoors. Hackers find fun in breaking things.

Fourth, the use of vulnerabilities:

For decent hackers, the vulnerabilities should be patched and for evil hackers, vulnerabilities should be used to destroy. Hackers' basic premise is "utilization of vulnerabilities". Hackers can use the vulnerabilities to do the following things:

1. Obtain system information:

Some vulnerabilities can leak system information, expose sensitive data, and further invade the system.

2. Intrusion system:

Can be used to enter through vulnerabilities into the system, or obtain internal information on the server, or completely become in charge of the server.

3. Looking for the next goal:

A victory means the emergence of the next target, hackers should make full use of the server they have been in charge as a tool to find and invade the next System.

4. Do some good things:

The decent hacker will complete the above work and will fix the loophole or notify the system administrator to do some things to maintain network security.

5. Do some bad things:

The evil hacker will do the above work. He will determine whether the server has value. If they have value, they will implant a Trojan or a back door on the server for the next visit. For those servers that don't have any value, they will never be merciless, and the system crash will make them feel infinitely happy.

This is just a basic introduction about hacking and we will discuss further in future about Hacking in detail. For now, we will start learning about kali Linux and Linux in detail along with a lot of tools that will start the hacking journey.

There are plenty of books on this subject on the market, thanks again for choosing this one! Every effort was made to ensure it is full of as much useful information as possible, please enjoy!

Chapter 1: The Hacking process & Kali Linux Installation

This chapter explains to us the hacking process that beginner hackers should master to get a good overview of hacking and its importance. Although being a little practical, this chapter will get you started and help you understand the basic things you need to know for becoming a professional hacker. We will also explain how to install a virtual machine and Kali Linux in this chapter. Let us start!

Essential things for a hacker

1) First, have a Basic English understanding:

Knowing English is critical for hackers, as most instructions made for them are now in English. Therefore, beginner hackers should try to read English materials, use English software, while paying attention to foreign network security at the same time. You may occasionally use foreign resources to master hacking methods and techniques.

2) Second, use and learn basic software:

The basic software cited here has two major components. One is the common computer commands we use every day, such as FTP, ping, net, etc., while the other is learning about primary hacking tools. Port and Vulnerability Scanners, Information Interception Tools, and password cracking tools. This software has many uses and functions. This book is going to introduce several popular software usage methods. After learning the basic principles, learners can choose either their own tools or create their own tools. Find the development guide for the software and write to make your signature hacking tools for a better understanding of the network structure.

3) Third, an elementary understanding of network protocol and working principle is a must:

The so-called "preliminary understanding" is to "get their own understanding on the topic" to understand the working principle of the network, because the knowledge involved in the agreement is complex, I mean very complex if you do in-depth research at the beginning, it is bound to/Will greatly dampen the enthusiasm for learning. Here I suggest that learners have a preliminary understanding of the TCP/IP protocol, especially how the network communicates and how information is exchanged when browsing the web, how the client browser applies for "handshake information," how the server "responses to handshake information" and "accepts requests."

4) Get to know several popular programming languages and scripts:

There is no requirement for learners to learn thoroughly, as long as you know the results of program executions. It is recommended that learners initially learn Python, ASP, and CGI scripting language, and have an elementary understanding of HTML, PHP, and Java, etc., you need to concentrate mainly on the "variables" and "array" parts of these languages because there is an inherent connection between languages. In a way, such that so long as you are proficient in one of them, other languages can come later. It is recommended to learn C language and HTML.

5) Get intimate with a web application:

Web applications include various servers' software daemons, such as wuftp, Apache, and other server backgrounds. There are various popular forums and e-communities on the Internet. Conditional learners should make their own computers into servers, and then install and run some forum code. After some test runs, they will be sensible to understand the working principle of the network, which is much easier than relying on theoretical learning. Try to do more with less work.

Some important concepts you need to master before hacking:

I. The Protocol

Networks are places where information is exchanged. All computers accessing the network can exchange information through a physical connection between devices. Physical equipment includes the most common cables, optical cables, wireless WAPs, and microwaves. However, merely possessing these physical devices does not enable information exchange. It is the same when the human body is not controlled by the brain, and the information exchange must have a software environment. This software environment is a set of rules that humans have implemented. It is called a protocol. With a protocol, different computers can use physical devices in accordance with the same protocol and do not cause mutual incomprehension.

This kind of agreement is very similar to Morse code. It can be changed in a simple way. However, if there is no control table, no one can understand what the content of a chaotic code is. The same is true for computers, which accomplish different missions through various pre-defined protocols. For example, the RFC1459 protocol enables IRC servers to communicate with client computers. Therefore, both hackers and network administrators must achieve the purpose of understanding the network operation mechanism through learning protocols.

Each protocol has been modified and used for many years. The newly generated protocols are mostly established based on the basic protocol. Therefore, the basic protocol has a relatively high-security mechanism. It is difficult for hackers to discover security problems in the protocol. However, for some new types of protocols, because of a short time and poor consideration, hackers for security reasons may also exploit them.

For community talk of network protocols, people think that the basic protocol used today has security risks at the beginning of the design. Therefore, no matter what changes are made to the network, if the network does not go under core changes, it is fundamentally impossible to impede any emergence of cyber hackers. However, this kind of hacking function is out of the confines of this book, and it is not covered here.

Second, the server and the client:

The most basic form of network service is several computers as clients, using a computer as a server where the individual client can send out requests to the server, then the server responds and completes the requested action, and finally, the server will return the execution result to the client computer. There are many such agreements. For example, the email server, web server, chat room server, etc. that we usually contact is all of this type. There is another kind of connection method where it does not need the server support, but directly connects two client computers; this makes the computers act as a server and client. Peer-to-peer completion of the connection and information exchange work. For example, the DCC transmission protocol falls into this category.

It can be seen from this that the client and the servers are the requesting application computer and the answering computer specified in various protocols, respectively. As a general Internet user, they all operate their own computers (clients) and send regular requests to the webserver to complete actions such as browsing the web, sending and receiving emails, and for hackers through their own computers (The client) attacks other computers (which may be clients or servers) to invade, destroy, and steal information.

Third, the system and system environment:

The operating system must be installed to operate the computer. The popular operating system is mainly UNIX, Linux, Mac, BSD, Windows2000, Windows95/98/Me, Windows NT, etc.. These operating systems run independently and have their own file management, memory management, process management, and other mechanisms. On the network, these different operating systems can be operated as servers or as clients, and they can exchange information through the protocol jobs.

Different operating systems and various applications constitute the system environment. For example, the Linux system can be used to configure the computer as a web server with Apache software. Other computers using the client can have the browser to get the website server for the viewer to read. The text information as Windows 2000 with Ftp software can be set up as a file server, through remote FTP login and can get various file resources on the system.

Fourth, IP address and port:

We go online and browse the web at the same time, send and receive an e-mail, voice chat, and many network services projects can be completed using various protocols, but the network is bigger than our computer. What do I do to find the computer I needed for my service? How to do so much work on one computer at the same time? Here we will introduce the IP address.

Computers connected with the Internet will have a unique IP address. An IP address is similar to a home address. Through various physical devices like network routers (without the need for newbies to understand). The computers in the network can easily do information exchange without any issues because their IP address is different; it is easier to find the target computer. Hackers, however, can make their computer's IP address change through specific methods, so any target server receives a request from the hacker. This is called Pseudo IP address. Servers will respond to the message sent from the pseudo IP address, thus causing network confusion. Hackers, of course, can find any surfers or servers based on IP addresses and attack them (think of real-time burglary) quickly.

Next, I will talk about the second question we talked about above: Why do I use multiple network services at the same time on one computer? It seems that New York City has eight gates. Distinct protocols will show in unique network services, and different network services will open via unique ports, much like City gates that help the client computer to complete its information transmission. In addition, if a web server has multiple network services open at the same time, it has to open a few different ports (city gates) to accommodate multiple and distinct client requests.

The back door that is often heard of on the Internet means that the hacker has opened up a network service on the server through specialized functions. The service hackers use to specifically complete their goals, and this will open with a new port. With this kind of service, regular internet users and administrators easily discover ports. These hidden ports are called a back door.

Each computer can open 65,535 ports. We can assume to develop at least 65,535 unique network services, but in fact, this number is very large. The network often uses dozens of service agreements, such as browsing web clients. Both port and server use port 80. For IRC chat, port 6667 is used on the server, and port 1026 is used on the client.

5) Vulnerabilities:

Vulnerabilities are situations that are not considered in the program. For example, the simplest "weak password" vulnerability means that the system administrator forgot to block accounts in some network applications. The Perl program vulnerability maybe because of the design of the programmers. When the program considers the imperfect situation, the code segment that causes the program to be executed is overwhelmed. The overflow vulnerability belongs to the original design of the system or program, without pre-reserving sufficient resources, and in the future, the program is used. The resulting resources are insufficient; the special IP packet bomb is actually an error when the program analyzes some special data, etc...

Overall, the loophole is a human negligence in the design of the program, which is almost improbable to avoid in any program, the hacker uses all kinds of loopholes to attack the network. The word "network security" at the beginning of this chapter is actually the meaning of "vulnerability." Hackers use vulnerabilities to complete various intrusion to get the ultimate result. In fact, hackers are really defined as "the person looking for vulnerabilities." They are not cyber-attackers for fun but are obsessed with getting in through other people's programs and looking for vulnerabilities every day. It is, to a certain extent, the hacker is the "good people." They are committed to this line in pursuit of perfection and establishment of a secure Internet, but only because some hackers or simply hackers often exploit aggressive vulnerabilities. In recent years, people have become scared of hackers.

6. Encryption and Decryption:

As an explanation of "Agreement," I cited "because of the problem of the grassroots of network design..." simply saying that this problem is to allow all users of Internet participating in information exchange, creating certain businesses, sharing personal privacy on the Internet will be exposed to participate in information sharing, and thus for certain businesses, the transmission of personal privacy on the Internet will be exposed to the public. Credit Cards, personal emails, etc. has the potential to be accessed by others through monitoring or interception. How can we make this information safe? The reader may have "World War II" thought of as spy war as the participating countries used the telegram to encrypt codes. Only the receiver who knows the password can decode the message. This ancient encryption method that still has its vitality in the modern network. The information processed by encryption is going through the network. No matter who gets the document, so long as they do not have a password, it is still in vain.

The longest use on the network is to set a personal password, use DES encryption lock, these two encryption methods can complete the user login system, website, email mailbox, and protection information package, and the work that hackers want to do is through loopholes. The brute force guessing, the reverse application of the encryption algorithm and other methods to obtain the plaintext of the encrypted file, some people use the "magic height one foot, and the road high one" is used here, it is indeed appropriate! Encryption methods on the network and systems that require password verification are emerging, and hackers are constantly looking for ways to break these systems.

It can be said that "vulnerabilities" and "decryption" are two completely different hacking fields. The preference of diverse learners for them will directly affect the types of hackers that they will become in the future, so the choices they make between them should be based on personal preferences, and this book will focus on learning about the "vulnerabilities."

Seventh, Trojan horse:

Trojan horse is an application designed and programmed by the programmer's intentional design. However, the operation of the Trojan horse, whether or not the user understands it, is not endorsed. According to some people's knowledge, viruses are a special case of Trojan horses: they can be spread to another program. They are also converted into Trojan horses. According to another person's understanding, viruses that are not intentionally causing any damage are not Trojan horses. Regardless of how people define it, in the end, many people only use "Trojan horses" to describe malicious programs that cannot be copied in order to distinguish Trojan horses from viruses.

Commonly Used Hacker Software Classifications

1. Prevention:

This is from a class of software involved in security perspectives, like firewalls, virus checking software, system process monitors, port management programs, etc., all of these belong to such software. This type of software maximizes and raises security and personal privacy for computer users and will not be compromised by hackers. Network servers give great importance to the needs of such software. Log analysis software, system intrusion software, etc. helps administrators in maintaining servers and track hackers who invade the system.

Second, information collection:

Information collection software types include port, vulnerability, and weak password scanning, and other scanning software, as well as monitoring, interception of information packets, and any spyware application, most of which belong to the software is also true and evil. That is to say, regardless of decent hackers, evil hackers, system managers, and ordinary computer users, user-like software can accomplish different purposes. In most cases, hacker-like software is more frequent because they rely on such software to scan the server in all directions, get more information about the server, and get a better understanding of the server. In order to carry out hacking.

3 Trojans and worms:

This software is different, but they work very much the same way, they are both virus-hidden and destructive, and such that this application is workable by the people with control or setup prior via well-designed procedures, but they do need a certain amount of work. Of course, this application is programmable for the use by system administrators as a remote management tool for servers.

4. Floods

The so-called "flood," that is, information garbage bombs, can cause the target server to overload and crash through a large number of garbage requests. In recent years, DOS distributed attacks have become popular on the network. Flood software may be used as a mail or chat bomb. These "fool" software has been streamlined and programmed by network security enthusiasts. Also, the software is often used in the hands of "pseudo-hackers" accused at the beginning of this book.

V. Password cracking:

The most practical way to ensure network security is to count on the cryptosystem of various encryption algorithms. Hackers have the ability to easily get ciphertext of the password file, but if there is an encryption algorithm, they still cannot obtain the real password. Therefore, the use of a password cracking application is imperative; using a computer with high-speed computing capabilities, software like these use dictionary password or an exhaustive way to restore the encrypted essay.

6. Deception:

When you need to get the plaintext password mentioned above, hackers need to perform encryption algorithm restoration on the ciphertext, but if it is a complicated password, it is not so simple to crack. However, is it more convenient to let the person who knows the password directly tell the prototype of the hacker password? Deception software is designed to accomplish this.

7. Camouflage:

The ISP and the server will record all kinds of processes and actions on the network. If the hacker's action is not performed after a good camouflage, it is easily tracked by any security technology, leading straight back to the hacker. So disguising own IP address and any identifying information is essential for hacker's compulsory course, but to use any camouflage technology requires deep expertise of the network. This kind of software is used when there is no solid foundation at the beginning.

The fourth important section you need to master is learning the basic environment of hackers.

First, they find the right operating system:

We usually hear hackers love Linux because Linux provides a far more flexible operation option with more powerful functions compared to Windows. Examples of these functions are the forgery of IP addresses, it is easy to write special IP header information using the Linux system, but it is almost impossible under Windows system. However, Linux also has its shortcomings. The commands in this system are complex and complicated, which makes it not **convenient** for new users. Individual learners will not be open to give up "comfortable" Windows, give up wonderful computer games and convenient operation, and go all out to hacker learning. In addition, new hackers get used to the Windows system as most of the knowledge of the network is to be learned there. Relative to the Linux system, the hacking software under the Windows platform is not infrequent. In addition, by installing the package, the Windows system can also be debugged. The amount of procedures, so the beginner hacker does not have to start with Linux.

This book uses the platform Kali Linux because, for individual users, NT or 2000 is a little more demanding - system configuration requirements are too high. However, the use of 95 or 98 lacks some of the necessary functions - NET, TELNET commands are not perfect. However, most of the contents of this book will evaluate vulnerabilities, starting from a remote server, so it really is not needed to learn Kali Linux operating system.

Second, the commonly used software:

If you are using a Kali Linux, then good news for you – you do not have to install extra software, because the hacking knowledge we will meet depends on the commands and built-in software provided by the system and can be done easily. Aside from the basic operating system, learners need to install a variety of scanners and get better Trojan software, monitoring software, and so on. When needed, readers may choose to install software above and learn how to use them, but I want to tell you that for all kinds of bombs, as well as a variety of hacking software on the network, after learning this book, you can if you make your own and develop it yourself, there will be no need of using software written by others when you have one developed by yourself.

For the scanner and monitoring software, I give the following suggestions, and the software will be described in detail later in the book:

All three of these software's are free and powerful. Like Nmap and Metasploit is a domestic software, it integrates a different scanning option that supports both console and graphical interface operations, as well as detailed vulnerability instructions. For beginners learning to hack these tools, are more than enough.

Third, additional tools:

If you are able to install the tools above, it would be of huge help to learn to jack; of course, the following software is mainly to acquire additional content and for the "second part" learning to pave the way, so it doesn't hinder the study of this book.

1. Background server:

A background service program with some application on the network can be programmed to make the computer like a small server to learn corresponding network applications and makes it easy to understand mechanical work internally, in turn, immensely improve its own server's perceptual knowledge, while also being able to monitor the data on its own server when the server is activated. If another hacker was to attack, you can clearly document the other party's attack process, which a beginner can learn more hacking methods. For this book, we mainly introduce scripting language vulnerabilities such as Perl and ASP, so we can install an IIS or HTTPD. Then set up Active Perl to make your own server to have the ability to compile CGI and pl scripts. There is also a benefit to using your own server. You save a lot of online time by putting all the processes of learning and finding vulnerabilities on your own computer, saving you money and poses no danger to any network.

2 C language compilation platform

In the future, when learning to hack, you will encounter many "problems of your own." Others may not notice these problems on the network, so you cannot find the corresponding program. At this time, it is a matter of developing the devices by yourself, so setting up Borland C++ will make it easier. Through this compiler, learners can learn both the C language and some of the small programs listed later in this book to create a Tool library.

Fourth, the classification of network security software

Now let us look at the kinds of network security applications because, as a learning hacker, knowledge is two interrelated processes: learning how to hack while preventing a hack is vital.

1. Firewall:

The most common security application set up on any network. The firewall has both hardware and software. Most readers may see software firewalls. Its functions are mainly to filter spam (this is to make sure that your system will not be bomb attacked), to prevent any intrusions, whether by employing worms or hacking, to elevate the system's privacy to protect sensitive data, to monitor system resources in real-time, to prevent system crashes, and to maintain databases regularly. Backing up the main information... The firewall can patch vulnerabilities any system may have, leaving the hacker no chance even to try. In addition, for enterprises with LANs, firewalls can limit the opening of system ports and prohibit specific network services (to prevent Trojans).

2. Detection software:

The internet has a device for clearing a hacker program. The application, however, is combined with the Firewall and anti-virus software installed. If Trojans and worms are detected in the system and cleared, the software, in order to ensure there is no system infringement, it will automatically protect the hard disk data, automatically maintains the registry file, detect the content of the code, and monitor the open status of the system port. If the

31

user wants, they can set up a script in the software to shield a specified port (this function is the same as the firewall).

3. Backup tools:

These are applications meant to make a copy of the data in a server, which helps to update the data at the time of development, so even if and when a hacker destroys the database on the server, the software can completely repair the received intrusion data in a short time. In addition, for individual users, this kind of software can do a full image backup of the hard drive that, in the event of a system crash, users can restore the system to its original state at a certain point. An example of this is a software called Ghost.

4. Log records, analysis tools:

For a server, the log file is quintessential, as this is the tool that helps the administrator to check what requests the server has been receiving and where it was sent. This allows administrators to know when they have been hacked definitively, and with the help of the log analysis software, they can easily set up trackers for any intrusion, find where the hacker entered the system, and then find the hacker's location this way. For this very reason, hackers have to learn how to do IP address masquerading, server hopping, and clearing log files after hacking a server.

Installing a Virtual Machine

People must be prepared for everything. Hackers are no exception. Before hackers invade other computers on the Internet, they need to do a series of preparations, including installing virtual machines on computers, preparing commonly used tools, and mastering common ones.

Whether it is an attack or training, hackers will not try to use a physical computer, but build a virtual environment in a physical computer, that is, install a virtual machine. In a virtual machine, hackers can intuitively perform various attack tests and complete most of the intrusion learning, including making viruses, Trojans, and implementing remote control.

A virtual machine is a computer system that is simulated by software and mimics a system with complete hardware functionality and functions as an independent environment. The work that can be done on the physical machine can be implemented in the virtual machine. Because of this, more and more people are using virtual machines.

When you create a new virtual machine on a computer, you need to use part of the hard disk and memory capacity of the physical machine as the hard disk and memory capacity of the virtual machine. Each virtual machine has its own CMOS, hard drive, and operating system. Users can partition and format the virtual machine, install operating systems and application software, just like a physical machine.

The Java Virtual Machine is an imaginary machine that is typically implemented by software simulation on a real computer. The Java virtual machine has its own imagined hardware, such as processors, stacks, registers, etc., and has a corresponding instruction system. The Java virtual machine is mainly used to run programs edited by Java. Because the Java language has cross-platform features, the Java virtual machine can also directly run programs edited in Java language in multiple platforms without modification. The relationship between the Java virtual machine and Java is similar to the relationship between Flash Player and Flash.

There may be users who think that the virtual machine is just an analog computer, and at most, it can perform the same operations as a physical machine, so it does not have much practical significance. In fact, the biggest advantage of a virtual machine is virtualization. Even if the system in the virtual machine crashes or fails to run, it will not affect the operation of the physical machine. In addition, it can be used to test the latest version of the application or operating system. Even if the installation of the application with the virus Trojan is no problem because the virtual machine and the physical machine are completely isolated, the virtual machine will not leak in the physical machine data.

VMware is a well-known and powerful virtual machine software that allows users to run two or more windows and Linux systems simultaneously on the same physical machine. Compared with the "multi-boot" system, VMware adopts a completely different concept. Multiple operating systems of a physical machine can only run one of the systems at the same time. The switching system needs to restart the computer, but VMware is different. It is the same. Multiple operating systems can be run at any time, thus avoiding the hassle of rebooting the system.

The VMware installer can be downloaded from some common resource offering sites such as filehippo.com. After downloading the VMware installer, you can extract and install it. After the installation is successful, the corresponding shortcut icon will be displayed on the desktop.

The following describes the steps to create a new virtual machine in VMware.

STEP01:

Start VMware Workstation by using the GUI interface.

STEP02:

Select a new virtual machine

STEP03:

Select the configuration type

STEP04:

Select to install the operating system later

STEP05:

Select the guest operating system

STEP06:

Set the virtual machine name and installation location

STEP07:

Specify virtual machine disk capacity

STEP08:

Click the "Finish" button

Installation of Kali Linux

Nowadays, the installation process of Linux has been very "fast," and the installation of the entire system can be completed with a few mouse clicks. The installation of the Kali Linux operating system is also very simple. This section describes the detailed process of installing Kali Linux to the hard drive, USB drive. We will explain how to upgrade tools in the next section.

Installing to a hard drive is one of the most basic operations. The implementation of this work allows users to run Kali Linux without using a DVD. Before you install this new operating system, you need to do some preparatory work. For example, where do you get Linux? What are the requirements for computer configuration? ... These requirements will be listed one by one below.

- The minimum disk space for Kali Linux installation is 8GB. For ease of use, it is recommended to save at least 25GB to save additional programs and files.
- The memory is preferably 512MB or more.

The official website provides 32-bit and 64-bit ISO files. This book uses 32-bit as an example to explain the installation and use. After downloading the ISO file, burn the image file to a DVD. Then you can start to install Kali Linux to your hard drive.

(1) Insert the installation CD into the CD-ROM of the user's computer, restart the system, and you will see the interface

(2) This interface is the guiding interface of Kali, and the installation mode is selected on this interface. Selecting the Graphical Install here will display an interface.

3) Select the default language of the installation system in this interface as English, and then click the Continue button then the next interface will be shown.

(4) In the interface selection area is "Your country," and then click the "Continue" button, the next interface will be displayed.

(5) Select the keyboard mode as "English" in this interface, and then click "Continue" button, the next interface will be displayed.

(6) This interface is used to set the hostname of the system. Here, the default hostname Kali is used (users can also enter the name of their own system). Then click the "Continue" button, the next interface will be displayed.

(7) This interface is used to set the domain name used by the computer. The domain name entered in this example is kali.example.com. If the current computer is not connected to the network, you can fill in the domain name and click the "Continue" button. The next interface will be displayed.

(8) Set the root user password on this interface, and then click the "Continue" button, the next interface will be displayed.

(9) This interface allows the user to select a partition. Select "Use the entire disk" here, and then click the "Continue" button, the next interface will be displayed.

(10) This interface is used to select the disk to be partitioned. There is only one disk in the system, so the default disk is fine here. Then click the "Continue" button, the next interface will be displayed.

(11) The interface requires a partitioning scheme, and three schemes are provided by default. Select "Place all files in the same partition (recommended for beginners)" and click the "Continue" button, the next interface shown will be displayed.

(12) Select "Partition setting ends and writes the changes to disk" in the interface, and then click "Continue" button, the next interface will be displayed. If you want to modify the partition, you can select "Undo the modification of the partition settings" in this interface to re-partition.

(13) Select the "Yes" checkbox on this interface, and then click the "Continue" button, the next interface will be displayed.

(14) Start installing the system now. Some information needs to be set during the installation process, such as setting up network mirroring. If the computer on which the Kali Linux system is installed is not connected to the network, select the "No" checkbox on this screen and click the "Continue" button. Select the "Yes" checkbox here, and the next interface will be displayed.

(15) Set the HTTP proxy information on this interface. If you do not need to connect to the external network through the HTTP proxy, just click the "Continue" button, the next interface will be displayed.

(16) After the scanning mirror site is completed, you can go to the next option

(17) In the country where the image is selected, select "Your country" and click "Continue" button, the next interface will be displayed.

(18) The interface provides 7 mirror sites by default, and one of them is selected as the mirror site of the system. Select mirrors.163.com here, then click the "Continue" button, the next interface will be displayed.

(19) Select the "Yes" checkbox on this interface, and then click the "Continue" button, the next interface will be displayed.

(20) The installation will continue at this time. After the installation process is finished, Kali Linux login screen will appear.

Installing kali Linux using a USB drive

The Kali Linux USB drive provides the ability to permanently save system settings, permanently update and install packages on USB devices, and allows users to run their own personalized Kali Linux.

Create a bootable Live USB drive for the Linux distribution on the Win32 Disk Imager, which includes continuous storage for Kali Linux. This section describes the steps to install Kali Linux to a USB drive.

Installing an operating system onto a USB drive is a bit different from installing to a hard drive. Therefore, you need to do some preparation before installing it. For example, where do you get Linux? USB drive format? What is the size of the USB drive? These requirements will be listed one by one below.

After the previous preparations are completed, you can install the system. The steps to install Kali Linux onto a USB drive are as follows.

(1) Insert a formatted and writable USB drive into the Windows system. After inserting, the display next interface is shown.

2) Start Win32 Disk Imager, the startup interface is shown. In the Image File location, click the icon to select the location of the Kali Linux DVD ISO image and select the USB device where Kali Linux will be installed. The device in this example is K. After selecting the ISO image file and USB device, click the Write button to write the ISO file to the USB drive.

(3) Use the UNetbootin tool to make the device K a USB boot disk. Launch the UNetbootin tool, and the next interface will be displayed.

(4) Select the "Disc Image" checkbox in this interface, then select the location of the ISO file and set the Space used to preserve files across reboots to 4096MB.

(5) Select the USB drive, the USB drive in this example is K, and then click the "OK" button; it will start to create a bootable USB drive.

(6) After the creation is completed, the next interface will be displayed.

(7) At this point, the USB drive is created successfully. In the interface, click the "Restart Now" button, enter the BIOS boot menu and select USB boot, you can install the Kali Linux operating system.

When users use it for a while, they may be dissatisfied with working in a system that does not change at all but is eager to upgrade their Linux as they would on a Windows system. In addition, Linux itself is an open system, new software appears every day, and Linux distributions and kernels are constantly updated. Under such circumstances, it is very important to learn to upgrade Linux. This section will introduce Kali updates and upgrades.

Updating and Upgrading Kali Linux

The specific steps for updating and upgrading Kali are as follows.

(1) Select "Application" | "System Tools" | "Software Update" command in the graphical interface, and the next interface will be displayed.

(2) The interface prompts to confirm whether the application should be run as a privileged user. If you continue, click the "Confirm Continue" button, the next interface will be displayed.

(3) The interface shows that a total of packages need to be updated. Click the "Install Update" button to display the interface.

(4) This interface shows the packages that the update package depends on. Click the "Continue" button to display the interface.

(5) From this interface, you can see the progress of the software update. In this interface, you can see a different status of each package. Among them, the package appears behind the icon, indicating that the package is downloading; if displayed as icons

indicate the package has been downloaded; if there is at the same time and icon, then, after you install this package, you need to reboot the system; these packages are installed once successful, it will appear as an icon. At this point, click the "Exit" button and restart the system. During the update process, downloaded packages will automatically jump to the first column. At this point, scrolling the mouse is useless.

(6) After restarting the system, log in to the system and execute the lsb_release -a command to view all version information of the current operating system.

7) From the output information, you can see that the current system version is 2.2.1. The above commands apply to all Linux distributions, including RedHat, SuSE, and Debian. If you only want to view the version number, you can view the /etc/issue file. Execute the command as follows:

root@kali:~# cat /etc/issueKali GNU/Linux 2.2.1\n \l

A Hacking Roadmap

If a hacker wants to attack a target computer, it cannot be done by DOS commands. It also needs some powerful intrusion tools, such as port scanning tools, network sniffing tools, Trojan making tools, and remote-control tools. This section will briefly introduce the intrusion tools commonly used by hackers.

a) Port scanning

The port scanning tool has the function of scanning the port. The so-called port scanning means that the hacker can scan the information of the target computer by sending a set of port scanning information. These ports are intrusion channels for the hacker. Once the hacker understands these ports, the hacker can invade the target computer.

In addition to the ability to scan the open ports of a computer, the port scan tool also has the ability to automatically detect remote or target computer security vulnerabilities. Using the port scan tool, users can discover the distribution of various TCP ports on the target computer without leaving traces. In addition, the services provided to allow users to indirectly or directly understand the security issues of the target computer. The port scanning tools commonly used by hackers are SuperScan and X-Scan.

b) Sniffing tool

A sniffing tool is a tool that can sniff packets on a LAN. The so-called sniffing is to eavesdrop on all the packets flowing through the LAN. By eavesdropping and analyzing these packets, you can peek at the private information of others on the LAN. The sniffing tool can only be used in the local area network, and it is impossible to directly sniff the target computer on the Internet. The data sniffing tools commonly used by hackers are Sniffer Pro and Eiffel Web Detective.

3) Trojan making tool

As the name suggests, Trojan making tools are tools for making Trojans. Since Trojans have the function of stealing personal privacy information of the target computer, many junior hackers like to use Trojans to make Trojans directly. The Trojan creation tool works basically the same way. First, the tool is used to configure the Trojan server program. Once the target computer runs the Trojan server program, the hacker can use the Trojan tool to completely control the target computer of the Trojan.

The operation of the Trojan making tool is very simple, and the working principle is basically the same, so many junior hackers favor it. Trojan horse making tools commonly used by hackers are "glacial" Trojans and bundled Trojans.

4) **Remote control tools**

Remote control tools are tools with remote control functions that can remotely control the target computer, although the control methods are different (some remote-control tools are remotely controlled by implanting a server program, and some remote-control tools are used to directly control the LAN, and all computers in the middle), but once the hacker uses the remote-control tool to control the target computer, the hacker acts as if he/she were sitting in front of the target computer. The remote-control tools commonly used by hackers are network law enforcement officers and remote control.

Hacking Target Computers

On the Internet, to prevent hackers from invading their own computers, it is necessary to understand the common methods of hacking target computers. The intrusion methods commonly used by hackers include data-driven attacks, illegal use of system files, forged information attacks, and remote manipulation. The following describes these intrusion methods.

1) A data-driven attack

A data-driven attack is an attack initiated by a hacker who sends or copies a seemingly harmless unique program to a target computer. This attack allows hackers to modify files related to network security on the target computer, making it easier for hackers to invade the target computer the next time. Data-driven attacks mainly include buffer overflow attacks, format string attacks, input verification attacks, synchronous vulnerability attacks, and trust vulnerability attacks.

2) Forgery information attack

Forgery information attack means that the hacker constructs a fake path between the source computer and the target computer by sending the forged routing information so that the data packets flowing to the target computer are all passed through the computer operated by the hacker, thereby obtaining the bank account in the data packet—personal sensitive information, such as passwords.

3) Information protocol

In a local area network, the source path option of the IP address allows the IP packet to choose a path to the target computer itself. When a hacker attempts to connect to an unreachable computer A behind a firewall, he only needs to set the IP address source path option in the sent request message so that one of the destinations addresses of the packet points to the firewall, but the final address points to Computer A. The message is allowed to pass when it reaches the firewall because it points to the firewall instead of computer A. The IP layer of the firewall processes the source path of the packet and sends it to the internal network. The message arrives at the unreachable computer A, thus achieving a vulnerability attack against the information protocol.

4) Remote operation

Remote operation means that the hacker launches an executable program on the target computer. The program will display a fake login interface. When the user enters the login information such as account and password in the interface, the program will save the account and password then transfer it to the hacker's computer. At the same time, the program closes the login interface and prompts the "system failure" message, asking the user to log in again. This type of attack is similar to a phishing website that is often encountered on the Internet.

5) LAN security

In the local area network, people are one of the most important factors of LAN security. When the system administrator makes a mistake in the configuration of the WWW server system and the user's permission to expand the user's authority, these mistakes can provide opportunities for the hacker. Hackers use these mistakes, plus the command of a finger, netstat, etc., to achieve intrusion attacks.

Resending an attack means that the hacker collects specific IP data packets and tampers with the data, and then resends the IP data packets one by one to spoof the target computer receiving the data to implement the attack.

In the LAN, the redirect message can change the router's routing list. Based on these messages, the router can suggest that the computer take another better path to propagate the data. The ICMP packet attack means that the hacker can effectively use the redirect message to redirect the connection to an unreliable computer or path or to forward all the packets through an unreliable computer.

6) Vulnerability attack

A vulnerability attack for source path selection means that the hacker transmits a source path message with an internal computer address to the local area network by operating a computer located outside the local area network. Since the router will trust this message, it will send an answer message to the computer located outside the LAN, as this is the source path option requirement for IP. The defense against this type of attack is to properly configure the router to let the router discard packets that are sent from outside the LAN but claim to be from internal computers.

7) Ethernet broadcast attack

The Ethernet broadcast attack mode refers to setting the computer network card interface to promiscuous, to intercept all the data packets in the local area network, analyze the account and password saved in the data packet, and steal information.

UNIX

On the Internet, servers or supercomputers on many websites use the UNIX operating system. The hacker will try to log in to one of the computers with UNIX, get the system privilege through the vulnerability of the operating system, and then use this as a base to access and invade the rest of the computer. This is called Island-hopping.

A hacker often jumps a few times before attacking the final destination computer. For example, a hacker in the United States may log in to a computer in Asia before entering the FBI network, then log in to a computer in Canada, then jump to Europe, and finally from France. The computer launches an attack on the FBI network. In this way, even if the attacked computer finds out where the hacker launched the attack, it is difficult for the administrator to find the hacker. What's more, once a hacker gains the system privileges of a computer, he can delete the system log when exiting and cut the"vine."

In almost all protocol families implemented by UNIX, a well-known vulnerability makes it possible to steal TCP connections. When a TCP connection is being established, the server acknowledges the user request with a response message containing the initial sequence number. This serial number has no special requirements, as long as it is unique. After the client receives the answer, it will confirm it once, and the connection will be established. The TCP protocol specification requires a serial number of 250,000 replacements per second, but the actual replacement frequency of most UNIX systems is much smaller than this number, and the number of next replacements is often predictable, and hackers have this predictable server initial. The ability of the serial number allows the intrusion attack to be completed. The only way to prevent this attack is to have the starting sequence number more random. The safest solution is to use the encryption algorithm to help generate the initial sequence number. The resulting extra CPU load is now the hardware speed. It can be ignored.

On UNIX systems, too many files can only be created by super users, and rarely by a certain type of user. This makes it necessary for system administrators to operate under root privileges. This is not very safe. Since the primary target of hacking is the root, the most frequently attacked target is the super user's password. Strictly speaking, the user password under UNIX is not encrypted. It is just a key for encrypting a common string as a DES algorithm. There are now a number of software tools for decryption that use the high speed of the CPU to search for passwords. Once the attack is successful, the hacker becomes an administrator on the UNIX system. Therefore, the user rights in the system should be divided, such as setting the mail system administrator management, and then the mail system mail administrator can manage the mail system well without superuser privileges, which makes the system much safer.

Chapter 2: Wireless Hacking and penetration testing

This chapter in detail will explain about the wireless attacks that can be done using kali Linux. First of all, we will give a brief overview about different wireless network analysis tools that are famously known to analyze the network packets. And in the next section, we will go through Aircrack-ng a kali linux wireless tool that can be used to crack wifi passwords of certain encryptions.

In this day and age, almost everyone is connected to the Internet. Especially if you're on the road a lot, you want wireless signals everywhere so you can do whatever you're doing. But in many cases, these wireless signals need to be authenticated before they can be used. Sometimes you may need the network urgently, but do not know its wireless password, this user may be very anxious. In Kali, as it happens, there are a number of tools available to crack the wireless network. This chapter describes the use of various penetration testing tools to carry out wireless network attacks.

What is Sniffing?

Sniffing is a process of acquiring wireless data packets by hacking tools and using them for malicious purposes. Sniffing is often called script kiddies method due to its easy acquiring of the information. Although websites and Applications have improved, their encryption abilities a lot of users can be tricked to give out their sensitive information like passwords and one-time passwords using sniffing techniques. Wireshark is a famous tool that can be used for wireless attacks.

Wireless network sniffer tool Kismet

If a wireless network penetration test is to be performed, all valid wireless access points must be scanned first. Just in time, Kali Linux offers Kismet, a wireless network sniffing tool. Use this tool to measure the surrounding wireless signal and view all available wireless access points. This section describes sniffing a wireless network using the Kismet tool.

Step 1:

Launch the Kismet tool. Execute the command as follows

 # kismet

Step 2:

The interface prompts you to run the Kismet tool using the root user. At this point, select Ok. Right after that, the interface prompts you to start the Kismet service automatically. Selecting "Yes" here.

Step 3:

The interface displays some information about setting up the Kismet service. Use the default settings here and select Start. The next interface shows if you want to add the undefined package resource now. Select Yes.

Step 4:

Specify the wireless network card interface and description information in the interface. In INTF, enter the wireless card interface. If your wireless card is already in listening mode, type WLAN0 or MON0. Other information can be left unadded. Then click the Add button.

Step 5:

The next interface displays information that is being sniffed for signals in the wireless network. When running for a certain amount of time, stop the modification. Click the Kismet menu option on the screen and select the Quit command. Clicking Kill in this interface stops the Kismet service and exits terminal mode.

Step 6:

In the Kismet is shutting down section of the above message, you will see that several log files have been closed. By default, log files will be saved in a directory called Root. In these log files, the time when the logs were generated is displayed. These times are very helpful when running Kismet many times or for a few days.

Let's analyze the data captured above. Switch to the / Root / Directory and use the ls command to view the log file generated above. Execute the command as follows:

root@kali:~# ls Kismet -2034344-23-9-4-1.*

From the output, you can see that there will be five log files with different suffix names. All the information generated by the Kismet tool is stored in these files.

alert: This file contains all warning information

gps xml: If the GPS source is used, the relevant GPS data is saved in the file

NETTXT: includes all collected text output information.

NETXML: includes data in all XML formats

PCAPDUMP: includes packets captured throughout the session.

Analyzing Text files for Kismet

In Linux, you can use a variety of text editor to open a nettxt file. Open the nettxt file using leafpad.

From this interface, you can see that the nettxt file contains a large amount of information, listing each wireless network scanned. Each wireless network has a label and lists each client connected to those wireless networks.

Aircrack-ng

Aircrack-ng is a WEP and WPA-PSK encryption tool based on the IEEE 802.11 protocol. This tool mainly uses two kinds of attack way to carry on Wep to break. One is the FMS attack, named after the researchers who discovered the WEP vulnerability. The other is the Korek attack, which is a statistical attack And this attack is much more efficient than the FMS attack. This section describes cracking a wireless network using Aircrack-ng.

Breaking the WEP encrypted wireless network

Wep protocols are a way of encrypting data that travels wirelessly between devices to prevent illegal users from eavesdropping or breaking into wireless networks. However, cryptanalysts have identified several weaknesses in Wep, which were eliminated by WPA in 2003 and replaced by WPA2. This section describes a wireless network that breaks WEP encryption.

Using Aircrack to crack a wireless network encrypted with WEP. The steps are as follows

(1) Use the airmon-ng command to see the wireless network interface on the current system. Execute the command as follows:

#airmon-ng

The output information indicates that there is a wireless network interface in the current system.

Output:

Interface   Chipset Driver

Wlan0   (you will get your driver name here)

(2) Try to change the mac address of the wifi system or device. Because the MAC address identifies the host's network, modifying the host's Mac address can hide the real Mac address.

You need to stop the interface before changing the MAC address. Execute the command as follows:

airmon-ng stop wlan0

Or you can even try the command

root@kali:~# ifconfig wlan0 down

After executing the above command, the WLAN0 interface stops. At this point, you can change the physical address also known as MAC and execute the command as follows:

root@kali:~# macchanger --mac 22:33:44:55:66:77 wlan0

Permanent MAC: 00:c1:39:76:05:6c (unknown)

Current MAC: 00:c3:40:77:05:6e (unknown)

New MAC: 22:33:34:34:23:67 (Hp Inc)

The output shows the permanent Mac address of the physical device and the current Mac address, and the new Mac address. You can see that the Mac address of the wlan1 interface has been modified.

Sometimes the SIOCSIFFFLAGS: Operation not possible to RF-kill error occurs when the wireless card is enabled using the airmon-ng Start Wlan0 command. That's because there's a software under Linux called RF-kill that turns off unused wireless devices like Wifi and Bluetooth to save on power. When the user uses these devices, RF-kill does not intelligently open automatically and needs to be unlocked manually. The user can execute the RFKILL list command to see all the devices, as follows

rfkill unblock all

After executing the above command, there is no information output. The above command indicates that all deactivated devices are deactivated.

(3) Use the airodump command to locate all available wireless networks in the vicinity. Execute the command as follows:

#airodump-ng wlan0

Output shows all available wireless networks in the vicinity. When you find the wireless router the user wants to attack, press control along with C to stop the attack and search.

You can see from the output that there are a number of parameters. The details are as follows

BSSID: Wireless Ip address

PWR: Signal Level reported by network card.

BEACONS: Notification Number issued wirelessly

Data: The number of Data packets captured, including broadcast packets.

/ S: Number of data packets captured per second in the last 10 seconds

Ch: Channel Number (obtained from Beacons).

Essid: refers to the so-called SSID number. It can be empty if the hidden SSID is enabled

Rate: represents the transfer Rate.

FRAMES: Number of data packets sent by the client.

(4) Use airodump-ng to capture a file that specifies a BSSID. Execute the command as follows.

The options commonly used for the airodump-ng command are shown below

- C: Specify the channel to be selected.

- W: Specify a file name to hold captured data

- BSSID: specifies the BSSID of the attack.

(5) Open a new terminal window and run the aireplay command. The Syntax Format for the aireplay command is as follows:

aireplay-ng -1 0 -a [BSSID] -h [our Chosen MAC address] -e [ESSID] [Interface] aireplay-ng -dauth 1 -a [BSSID] -c [our Chosen MAC address] [Interface]

root@kali:~# aireplay-ng -1 0 -a 23:A4:3E:23:5R:20 -h

(6) Use aireplay to send some traffic to the wireless router so that data can be captured. The Syntax format is as follows:

aireplay-ng 3 -b [BSSID] -h [Our chosen MAC address] [Interface]

root@kali:~# aireplay-ng -3 -b 16:E6:4R:AC:FB:20 -h

The output is to use ARP Requests to read ARP Requests, at this point back to the airodump-ng interface, you can see the Test frame column in the number of rapid increase. After grabbing a certain number of wireless datagrams, the IVSX value is above 20,000 and can be cracked. If that doesn't work, wait for the data Frank Baumann to continue grabbing and try again.

(7) Using Aircrack to crack a password. Execute the command as follows:

aircrack -ng -b xx: mac wirelessatack-01.cap

From the output, you can see the KEY FOUND, that the password has been FOUND.

Attack WPS (Wi-Fi protected Setup)

WPS is a new Wi-Fi security settings standard introduced by the Wi-Fi consortium. The standard is mainly to solve the wireless network encryption authentication set too complicated steps of the disease. Because the user often because the setting step is too troublesome, do not make any encryption security settings, resulting in many security problems. So many people use WPS to set up wireless devices that can replace entering a long password phrase with a PIN or a button (PBC). When this feature is enabled, an attacker can attack WPS with a violent attack method. This section describes the various tools used to attack WPS.

Using deaver to break WPS. The steps are as follows.

(1) Insert the wireless card and use the IFCONFIG command to see if the wireless card has been inserted correctly. Execute the command as follows:

ifconfig

(2) Activate the Wireless Network Card to monitor mode. Execute the command as follows:

airmon -ng wlan0

Note: execute the above command to start listening mode, be sure to correctly identify the wireless card chip and driver. Otherwise, the wireless network card may cause the attack to fail.

(3) Attacking WPS. Execute the command as follows:

root@kali:~# reaver -i mono -b 14:E6:E4:DE:FB:20 -vv

Output:

From the above output, you can see that you are waiting for a signal to connect to the 14E4FB: 20 wireless router. And get the password by sending a PIN.

If no router is enabled and WPS is not enabled, the following information will appear:

. [!] WARNING: Failed to associate with 14:E6:E4:DE:FB:20 (ESSID: XXXX)

Fern wifi cracker

FERN WiFi Cracker is a great tool for testing wireless network security. This tool is used to attack Wi-Fi networks. The first step here is to use the FERN WIFI Cracker tool to attack WPS.

Attacking WPS with Wifite. The steps are as follows.

Start the Wifite tool and specify the use of common. Txt Password Dictionary. At the Command Line Terminal

root@kali:~# wifite -dict jesus.txt

This information shows the version of the WiFite tool, support for the platform, and the beginning of WiFite scanning. When scanning to the wireless network you want to jailbreak, press CTRL + C to stop scanning.

(2) Stop scanning the wireless network and the message shown below will be displayed:

From the above output, you can see that the scan has five wireless access points and three clients. In the output, a total of seven columns are displayed. Indicate wireless access point number, Essid number, channel, encryption mode, electrical power, whether to open WPS and client. If only one CLIENT is connected to the wireless access point, the CLIENT column appears to be CLIENT. If there are multiple client connections, clients is displayed.

(3) At this point, select the wireless access point to attack. Select the fifth wireless access point here and type "1". Then press enter to begin the attack, and the message is as follows:

select target numbers (1-5) separated by commas, or 'all': 1

GERIX WIFI CRACKER

Gerix Wifi Cracker is another graphical user interface wireless crack tool. This section describes how to use this tool to hack a wireless network and create fake access points

74

Previously, we introduced the manual use of Aircrack-ng to crack Wep and WPA / WPA2 encrypted wireless networks. For convenience, this section describes using the Gerix tool to automatically attack a wireless network. Using GERIX TO ATTACK WEP encrypted wireless networks. The steps are as follows

root@kali:/usr/share/gerix-wifi-cracker# python gerix.py

After executing the above command, the interface appears

(1) You can see from this interface that the Gerix database has been successfully loaded. At this point, switch to the Configuration tab with the mouse, a

(2)From the interface, you can see that there is only one wireless interface. Therefore, now we're going to do a configuration. Select Interface wlan1 in this interface and click the Enable / Disable Monitor Mode button to display the interface

(3) From this interface, you can see that WLAN1 has been successfully started in listening mode. Select MON0 with the mouse, click the Rescan networks button under the Select the target network and the interface appears

(4) From this interface you can see all the wireless networks near the scan. In this example, we selected a wireless network that attacks WEP encryption, and here we selected the Essid as the wireless network for Test. Then switch the mouse over to the WEP TAB,

(5) This interface is used to configure WEP related information. Click the General functionalities command to display the interface

(6) The interface shows how WEP can be attacked. Under functional assets in the interface, click the Start Sniffing and Logging button to display the interface

(7) The interface shows the wireless AP used to transfer data with Test. Then click the WEP Attacks (no-client) command

(8) Click the Start false access point Authentication on victim button on the screen and there is no output. Then click the Start the ChopChop attack button to display the interface

(9) The interface is the process of fetching the packet. When the wireless AP is captured, the Use this packet? At this point, the input y will begin to capture the data, generating a file named The. Cap File,

(10) Ask if you want to Use this packet? At Use this packet? After entering Y, will grab a large number of packets. When the number of packets captured reaches 20,000, click the Cracking tab to display the interface

(11) From this interface, we can see that the common time for cracking WEP encrypted passwords is 3 minutes.

Creating fake access points using Gerix

Using the Gerix tool, you can create and establish a fake access point (AP). Setting up a fake access point can trick the user into visiting the access point. Now, people tend to do this for convenience. Connect to open wireless access points for quick and easy e-mail or social networking. Here, we'll take a WEP encrypted wireless network as an example to create fake access points.

1) Launch the Gerix tool. Execute the command as follows:

root@kali:/usr/share/gerix-wifi-cracker# python gerix.py

Switch to the Configuration tab. Select the wireless interface in this interface and click the Enable / Disable Monitor Mode button. When the listening mode is successfully started, click the Rescan Networks button under the Select Target Network.

2) Of all the networks scanned, select a WEP encrypted network. Then click the Fake AP TAB, which displays the interface

From this interface, you can see that the default access point Essid is honeypot. Now Change Honeypot to personal network, and also change the channel of the wireless interface that will be attacked.

After the above information is set up, the other configurations will remain the default settings. Then click the Start Fake Access Point button to display the interface

3) When a user connects to the personal network AP created, the interface outputs the information shown below

17:32:34 Client 18:AB:56:F0:62:AF associated(WEP) to ESSID: "itsnetwork"

Jailbreaking wireless networks using Wifite

1) Some jailbreaking wireless network programs use the Aircrack-ng toolset and add a graphical interface or use text menus to

jailbreak wireless networks. This makes it easier for the user to use them without having to remember any commands. This section describes the use of the command-line tool Wifite to scan and attack wireless networks.

#wifite

Stop scanning the wireless network and the message shown below will be displayed. From the above information, you can see the scan to 13 wireless access points.

(2) Choose the target of attack. The second wireless access point selected here is encrypted in WEP MODE

select target numbers (1-13) separated by commas, or 'all': 2

Use the Easy-Creds tool to attack wireless networks

Easy-creds is a menu-style cracking tool. The tool allows users to open a wireless network card and can implement a wireless access point attack platform. Easy-creds can create a spoofing access point and run as a man-in-the-middle attack type to analyze a user's data flow and account information. It can recover accounts from SSL encrypted data. This section describes using the Easy-Creds tool to attack wireless networks.

(1) Start the Easy-Creds tool. Execute the command as follows:

root@localhost:~/easy-creds-master#./easy-creds.sh

(2) Choose pseudo-AP attack here, enter number 3. The information will be displayed:

Choice: 3

(3) Here you choose to use a static pseudo-AP attack, enter number 1. The following information will be displayed:

choice : 1

After setting up the above information, some programs will be started automatically. After a few seconds, several valid windows will open

(4) When a user connects to a Wifi access point, Easy-Creds automatically assigns an IP address to the client and has access to the Internet. If you access a secure web site on the Internet, the tool will remove SSL, remove the secure connection, and run in the background. Therefore, it is possible to read the user name and Password of a Web site logged in by the client

(5) Select data recovery from the main menu of Easy-Creds and enter number 4, as follows:

choice : 4

(6) After selecting data recovery, the information shown below will be displayed:

(7) Select here to analyze the ETTERCAP ECI file and enter number 3 to display the following information:

Enter the full path to your ETTERCAP. ECI LOG FILE: From the output, you can see where the ETTERCAP log file is saved.

(8)Enter ETTERCAP at this time. The full path of the ECI log file. All you need to do here is copy and paste the entire Ettercap path provided.

Here's how it works:

Enter the full path to your ettercap.eci log file: /root/easycreds-master/easy-creds-2019-07-24-1722/ettercap2019-07-24-1724.eci

Attack the router

All of the tools described above connect to a wireless network by cracking passwords directly. Because of all the devices in a wireless network environment, router is one of the most important devices. Usually the user in order to protect the router's security, usually will set a more complex password. Even some users may use the router's default user name and password. However, the router itself has some vulnerabilities. If the user finds it difficult to work with a complex password. At this point, the router can use its own vulnerability to carry out the attack. This section describes the use of the Routerpwn tool to implement an attack router.

From this interface, we can see many router manufacturers, such as D-Link, Huawei, Netgear and TP-Link. Select the manufacturer based on your target router, and select TP-Link here,

The interface shows support for 16 different types of TP-LINK routers and available vulnerabilities. The router vulnerability list displays the vulnerability date, vulnerability description information, and an option [SET IP] . This option is used to set the Ip of the destination router.

Take advantage of a web shell backdoor vulnerability to get the command line of a remote router (in this case, the Ip address of the router is 192.168.0.1)

(1) Click the [SET IP] button to bring up a dialog box.

2) In this dialog, enter the IP address of the router you want to attack. Then click the OK button.

(3) Enter the LOGIN router's username and password in this interface. The default username and Password for a router is admin. Then click the login button to display the interface.

(4)At this point, the interface can be executed to view some of the router information command, such as view process, network, routing table and NAT. Or simply click the button in the right sidebar to see the information. When executing commands in this interface, you need to enter a user name and password. The user name and password are those provided by the web shell backdoor vulnerability at Routerpwn (Osteam and 5up). For example, clicking the view network button displays the interface

(5) From the interface can see the router, all the connection network interface information, such as the interface Ip address, Mac address and transmission rate. If you want to view it by executing a command, type the IFCONFIG command in the instruction box. Then click the send button,

(6) When you click the send button in this interface, the output is the same

Arp spoof

ARPSPOOF is a very good ARP spoof source code program. Its operation does not affect the entire network communications, the tool by replacing the transfer of data in order to achieve the goal of deception. This section describes the use of the ARPSPOOF tool.

URL MANIPULATION ATTACK

The URL traffic operation is very similar to man-in-the-middle attack, which injects routing traffic to the Internet through the target host. This process will implement the attack through ARP injection. This section describes URL traffic manipulation attacks using the ARPSPOOF tool. Implementation of URL traffic operation attack using ARPSPOOF tool. The steps are as follows:

(1) Enable routing and forwarding. Execute the command as follows:

root@kali:~# echo 1 >> /proc/sys/net/ipv4/ip_forward

(2) Launch Arpspoof to attack the target system. The method of attack is the attacker (192.168.6.232) sends ARP packets to deceive the gateway (192.168.6.235) and the target system 192.168.6.232. The following spoofs the target system first, executing the command as follows:

root@kali:~# arpspoof -i eth0 -t 192.168.6.232 192.168.6.235

The output shows the packet sent by the attacker to the target host 192.168.6.232. 503946:8D represents the attacker's Mac address; 193fe5 represents 192.168.6.235's Mac address

Address. When the above process attack is successful, when the target host 192.168.6.232 sends data to the gateway 192.168.6.235, it will all be sent to the attacker 192.168.6.234

(3) Inject the attack gateway using ARPSPOOF. Execute the command as follows:

```
root@kali:~# arpspoof -i eth0 -t 192.168.6.232 192.168.6.235
```

The above output shows the packets sent by the attacker to gateway 192.168.6.232. When the attack is successful, the gateway 192.168.6.232 sends the information on the target system 192.168.6.235 to the attacker's host 192.168.6.234.

(4) If all of the above steps are successful, the attacker has control over the data transmitted between the gateway and the target host. Through the data received, the attacker can see the important information on the target system

PORT REDIRECTION ATTACK

Port Redirection is also called port forwarding or port mapping. The process of receiving a port packet (such as Port 80) and redirecting its traffic to a different port (such as port 8080). The benefits of implementing this type of attack are endless, as it redirects traffic to a specific port on a given device from a secure port to an unencrypted port. This section describes the use of Arpspoof for port redirection attacks. Implementation of port redirection attack using ARPSPOOF. The steps are as follows.

(1) Enable forwarding attacks. Execute the command as follows:

root@kali:~# echo 1 >> /proc/sys/net/ipv4/ip_forward

(2) Start the Arpspoof tool to inject traffic to the default network. For example, the Default Gateway address in this example is 192.168.6.232. Execute the command as follows:

root@kali:~# arpspoof -i eth0 192.168.6.232

(3) After executing the above commands on Kali Linux, there is no output. This is a bug in Kali 1.0.6 because the version of the DSNIFF package on the system is dsniff-2.4 B1 + debian-22

(4) Add a firewall rule for port redirection. Execute the command as follows:

root@kali:~# iptables -t nat -A PREROUTING -p tcp --destinationport 80 -j REDIRECT --to-port 8080

When the above settings are successful, when the user sends a request to Port 80 of Gateway 192.168.6.232, the request will be forwarded to the attacker's host as port 8080.

Capturing and Monitoring Wireless Network Data

Using the man-in-the-middle attack method, the Kali Linux operating system can be placed between the target host and the router. In this way, the user can capture all the data from the target host. This section describes how to capture and monitor wireless network data using the man-in-the-middle attack tool.

(1) Enable the router forwarding function. Execute the command as follows:

(2) Attack the host with the ARPSPOOF command. Execute the command as follows:

root@kali:~# arpspoof -i eth0 -t 192.168.6.232 192.168.6.235

Executing the above command tells 192.168.6.232(the target host) that the gateway's Mac address is 00. When the target host receives the message, it modifies the ARP entry in the ARP cache table. It does not stop automatically after you execute the above command. If you don't need to attack, press CTRL + C to stop the attack.

(3) View information about the target host's access URL address. Execute the command as follows:

root@kali:~# urlsnarf -i eth0

The output above shows the target host's access to the Internet

(4) Users can also use the Driftnet tool to capture images viewed by the target system. Execute the command as follows:

root@kali:~# driftnet -i eth0

After you execute the above command, a window will open. When the target host accesses a web page with a picture, it is displayed in that window.

(5) Now go to the target host and access the Internet to generate the capture information. For example, if you randomly access a Web page through a browser on the target host, the attack host will display the interface

(6) The interface displays all the images accessed on the target host. Users can now click on any of the images, which will be saved to the Kali Mainframe. The following message will appear under the DRIFTNET command:

root@kali:~# driftnet -i eth0

As can be seen from above, the images captured by driftnet are saved. The file names are driftnet-* . PNG, and these files are saved by default in the current directory.

(7) Users can view it using the image viewer that comes with Linux.

Penetration testing

We all know that professional hackers that are ethical are also called as penetration testers. They usually work for companies to make their security better and not prone to attacks. Penetration testing follows a certain strategy and guidelines just like any other IT methodology. We will just go through around it for some time.

Purpose, procedure and method of pen testing

As mentioned in the previous chapters the white-capped hacker is entrusted by the peddler to attack, so the target and scope of the attack can be limited according to the needs of the peddler. This type of attack based on the content of the agreement is called "penetration test". (Penetration Test, referred to as Pentest or PT). "Penetration Test" aims to discover information assets and Risks to provide appropriate risk management. Why do companies or organizations need penetration testing? When information systems go online to provide services, hackers will continue to try to attack, whether the system can stand the test, and through penetration testing, the business owners can:

* Understand the ways that intruders may use
• Information & Improper disclosure or tampering
• Network architecture design issues
 • Firewall setup issues
 • System and application vulnerabilities

• System and application setup issues

■ Understanding system and network security strengths

• How long it takes to evaluate an intruder with equal capabilities Time invasion success
• Assessment was met the extent of the impact of the invasion
• Assess the implementation of the safety policy

■ Understand weaknesses, enhance security

• Strengthen system and network security
• Reduce post-invasion losses Wiki (WiKi)

The claim for penetration testing is: By attacking computer systems, to discover possible security weaknesses in the system, Access to system, program features, or sensitive data. The general statement is: Use the hacker's point of view, technology, and tools to mimic the hacker's attack techniques against the target system, in order to identify weaknesses or vulnerabilities in the system, and provide customer repair suggestions as a means of system enhancement.

The scope of the penetration test when the hacker is interested in the organization, will find ways to enter the organization, as far as the attack is concerned, the target of the start is divided into small: to a single system: for example, a website that provides a specific service, Like a shopping site, its backend or has many supported systems However, the main attack limit is limited to the features offered on the shopping site, and this category is mostly part of the website penetration test.

■ Server:

For the penetration of specific devices or computers that provide one or more services, the pervasive method that can be used depends on the type of service provided by the server. The most commonly tested object.

■ Segment or host farm (serverfarm):

Sometimes the specific website or server is easy to implement due to the small attack area. However, the defense mechanism of each system may be uneven between hosts in the same segment. The vulnerability of the B host is used as a springboard to reach the attack A host. The goal of. So open section testing can identify potential vulnerabilities.

■ System-wide:

Test all relevant information systems of the organization. The concept is the same as the segment or host group. When the testable range is larger, the organization's security protection capability can be better seen.

■ Personnel safety:

Information systems or applications Software is usually handled by specialized information personnel. In the awareness of security, information personnel should be higher than the average staff. Look for objects with lower security awareness for social engineering to obtain basic (or even high-right) use rights, sometimes can invade the target system faster.

■ All institutions:

When the organization is open to testing all assets, this situation is most close to the hacker attack, but because the scope of penetration testing is too broad, it is relatively difficult to have a complete and comprehensive evaluation results, few institutions will handle all Infiltration testing of the organization. I think the penetration test should be

■ Health check is not an attack:

Penetration testing is to find out the existing weaknesses as early as possible. As a basis for improvement, the implementation of the penetration test must take into account the continuous operation of the system, and it is necessary to prepare the countermeasures for the system to stop the service in advance.

■ Is an audit, not a steal:

Penetration testing can confirm the organization's the degree of implementation of the communication security policy is an auditing behavior. After the penetration test is completed, the relevant information must be completely handed over to the entrusting party as a strategic reference for continuously improving the security of the communication.

■ Protection is the purpose of the test:

The weaknesses found in the penetration test; the tester must propose the corresponding protective measures for the client is involved.

The method for handling the penetration test operation is hereinafter referred to as Party A, and Party B is responsible for performing penetration test.

■ Black box:

Party B only knows the name or URL of the target to be tested. Other information must be collected by itself during the testing activity. Using the black box test, is testing the hacking skills of Party B, because this pattern is closest to the actual hacking attack.

■ White Box:

Party A will provide information on the target as much as possible, so that Party B can focus on finding the weaknesses (vulnerabilities) of the system under test, and use the white box test to test the system's security protection ability.

■ **Gray box:**

Of course, sometimes Party A is not then, the information of the system under test (such as the system developed by the outsourcing system) cannot provide the complete information of the target to be tested. Party B cannot obtain the system information in advance, but Party A still assists Party B to obtain the equivalent information as much as possible. The box is between the black box and the white box Test Methods.

■ **Double black box:**

Sometimes Party A wants to test as much as possible in the context of simulating hacking attacks. It is necessary not only to test the protection capabilities of the system, but also to test the alertness or resilience of its own personnel. Secretly entrusting Party B to conduct infiltration operations, relevant the personnel did not know the penetration test, and Party B could not get detailed information about the system under test. Therefore, both offensive and defensive sides are competing in the dark, so it is called a double black box (or double-blind) test.

■ Double white box:

As opposed to double black box, both sides know each other's existence, the main purpose is to assist Party B. Party A finds and confirms system vulnerabilities.

By this, we have completed our journey into kali Linux and its tools and will go on to discuss further more in our next module. Always remember that hackers are not theoretical. Hackers do things. So, after reading this make yourself ready to experiment things. All the Best!

Conclusion

Thank you for making it through to the end of *Penetration Testing: The Ultimate 2021 Guide about Hacking Process & Kali Linux Installation. Defend Yourself from Wireless Hacking.*, let's hope it was informative and able to provide you with all of the tools you need to achieve your goals whatever they may be.

The next step is to make these things apply in real practical hacking life.

After understanding the intrusion methods commonly used by hackers, it is not realistic to plan separate protection strategies for these methods. Therefore, users can only master the common protection strategies of personal computer security to ensure that the computer is in a relatively safe environment. Common PC protection strategies include: installing and upgrading anti-virus software, enabling firewalls, preventing Trojans and viruses, sharing folders, and regularly backing up important data.

The emergence of viruses has caused huge losses to computers on the Internet. These viruses can cause the system to fail to operate normally, and the system will be formatted, and data will be formatted. In order to prevent the harm caused by these viruses, users need to install anti-virus software on the computer and turn on real-time monitoring. In addition, due to the improvement of virus production techniques and means, new viruses are constantly appearing, so users need to upgrade anti-virus software in time so that anti-virus software can prevent new viruses on the Internet.

A firewall is a method of separating a computer's internal network from an external network. In fact, this is an isolation technique. A firewall is an access control scale that is executed when two internal and external networks communicate. It allows users' licensed computers and specific data to enter the internal network, preventing hackers on the external network from accessing and attacking themselves to the maximum extent network.

In order to prevent Trojans and viruses from invading the Internet, first, do not download unidentified software and programs, select a reputable download site to download the program, and then put the successfully downloaded software and programs in addition to the system partition. Other partitions need to use anti-virus software to scan downloaded programs before opening.

In addition, do not open e-mails and attachments of unknown origin to avoid the invasion of mail viruses or bundled Trojans.

Even if you download the attachment that came with the message, you need to scan it with anti-virus software.

On the Internet, some hackers use "phishing" methods to scam, such as creating fake websites or sending e-mails containing fraudulent information, thereby stealing online banking, online payment tools, credit card accounts, and passwords, and stealing funds from the account. In order to prevent phishing, users must make sure that the URL of the private information they enter is the real URL, not the phishing website. Do not enter it at will.

In the LAN, when users share files, there will be software vulnerabilities, and hackers will detect these vulnerabilities. Therefore, users must set the access password when setting up a shared folder. Unshare should be canceled as soon as sharing is not required. In addition, when setting up a shared folder, users must make the shared folder read-only and do not set the entire disk partition as shared.

The importance of data backup is unquestionable, and no matter how tightly the computer's preventive measures are made, it cannot completely prevent unexpected situations. If a hacker is fatally attacked, although the operating system and application software can be reinstalled, important data cannot be reinstalled, and only rely on daily backups. Therefore, even if you take very strict precautions, do not forget to back up your important data at any time and be prepared.

CPSIA information can be obtained
at www.ICGtesting.com
Printed in the USA
LVHW012256080721
692216LV00011B/580